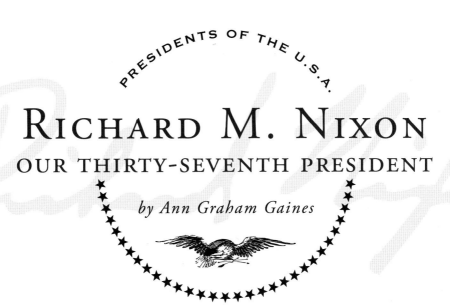

PRESIDENTS OF THE U.S.A.

RICHARD M. NIXON
OUR THIRTY-SEVENTH PRESIDENT

by Ann Graham Gaines

THE CHILD'S WORLD ®

PUBLISHED IN THE UNITED STATES OF AMERICA

THE CHILD'S WORLD®
1980 Lookout Drive • Mankato, MN 56003-1705
800-599-READ • www.childsworld.com

ACKNOWLEDGMENTS
The Child's World®: Mary Berendes, Publishing Director

The Creative Spark: Mary McGavic, Project Director and Page Production;
Shari Joffe, Editorial Director; Deborah Goodsite, Photo Research

The Design Lab: Kathleen Petelinsek, Design

Content Adviser: David R. Smith, Adjunct Assistant Professor of History,
University of Michigan–Ann Arbor

PHOTOS
Cover and page 3: White House Historical Association (White House Collection)
(Detail); White House Historical Association (White House Collection)

Interior: The Art Archive: 21 (Culver Pictures); Associated Press Images: 18
(Charles Harrity), 19, 22, 25, 28 (AP Photo); The Bridgeman Art Library: 26
(Private Collection, Peter Newark American Pictures); Corbis: 9, 17, 20, 27, 29,
35 and 39 (Bettmann), 11 (Corbis); Getty Images: 5 and 39 (Getty), 7, 23 (Time
& Life Pictures), 13 (Popperfoto), 16 and 38, 36 (AFP); The Granger Collection,
New York: 8 (Rue de Archives), 33 (The Granger Collection); The Image Works:
12 and 38, 14 (Topham), 24 (Charles Gatewood), 32, 34 (Mark Godfrey);
iStockphoto: 44 (Tim Fan); National Archives at College Park, Maryland: 31
(WHPO C6779-04), 37 (WHPO C9461-18), (Richard Nixon Presidential
Library and Museum Staff); Photo Researchers, Inc.: 10 (Arthur Schatz), 30
(NASA/Science Source); Richard Nixon Presidential Library and Museum: 4
(Richard Nixon Library and Birthplace Foundation); U.S. Air Force photo: 45;
Whittier College: 6 (Wardman Library, Special Collections).

LIBRARY OF CONGRESS CATALOGING-IN-PUBLICATION DATA
Gaines, Ann.
  Richard M. Nixon / by Ann Graham Gaines.
    p. cm. — (Presidents of the U.S.A.)
  Includes bibliographical references and index.
  ISBN 978-1-60253-065-2 (library bound : alk. paper)
  1. Nixon, Richard M. (Richard Milhous), 1913–1994—Juvenile literature. 2.
Presidents—United States—Biography—Juvenile literature. I. Title. II. Series.

E856G335 2008
973.924092—dc22
[B]

2008002304

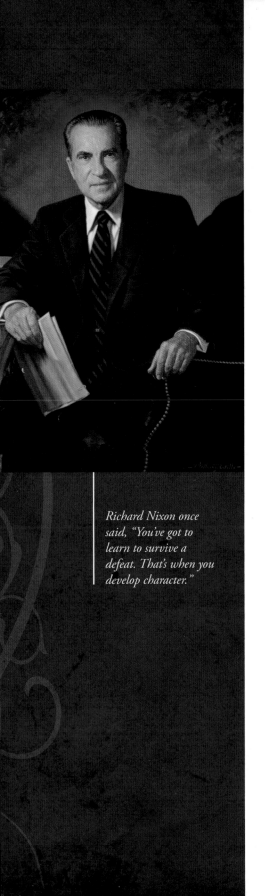

Richard Nixon once said, "You've got to learn to survive a defeat. That's when you develop character."

TABLE OF CONTENTS

YOUNG NIXON

Richard Nixon was the 37th president of the United States. He is the only president to **resign** from office. When he left the White House in 1974, many Americans did not think well of him. After all, he had decided to leave because of a **scandal.** Members of his staff had been accused of stealing papers from his political enemies, leaders of the **Democratic Party.** Nixon himself had tried to cover up what they did. But today he is also remembered with respect as an important leader in American foreign policy. His visits to the **Soviet Union** and China improved American relations with both those countries.

Richard Milhous Nixon was born on January 9, 1913, in Yorba Linda, a small town in California. His parents were Frank and Hannah Nixon. They were very different from each other. Frank Nixon was an

Richard M. Nixon rose from a humble background to become America's 37th president.

angry man who liked to argue. His main interest was **politics,** the work of the government. Hannah Nixon was sweet by nature. She was a quiet, patient, and religious woman whose life revolved around taking care of her children. Richard was the Nixons' second child. His older brother was named Harold. He would also have three younger brothers: Donald, Arthur, and Edward.

The Nixon family lived in Yorba Linda for the first ten years of Richard Nixon's life. They built a house there and planted a grove of lemon trees. But Frank

Nixon was born in this modest farmhouse in Yorba Linda, California. The house is now part of the Richard Nixon Presidential Library and Birthplace.

Nixon could never make much money as a farmer. In 1922, the family moved to the nearby town of Whittier, near Los Angeles. There Frank Nixon ran a gas station. Later he opened a grocery store. Unfortunately, he found little success in these business ventures. The family was always poor.

Richard Nixon first went to public school in Yorba Linda. He changed schools when his family moved to

Richard Nixon was a descendant of James Nixon, who arrived in Delaware from Ireland in 1753. One of Richard's ancestors fought in the American Revolution. Another fought in the Civil War.

Richard's father, Frank Nixon, never graduated from high school. When Frank was 12 years old, he had to find a job so he could help support his family.

Richard Nixon was the second of five sons. Shown here from left to right are Harold, Frank, Donald (on his mother's lap), Hannah, and Richard. The youngest boys, Arthur and Edward, had not yet been born when this photograph was taken.

Whittier. As a boy, Richard had a terrible time getting along with his classmates because he was shy. He also became angry if he didn't get his way. Because he wasn't popular, Richard pushed himself to earn good grades. He was always smart and worked hard.

When Richard Nixon was 12, tragedy struck his family. His little brother Arthur died from tuberculosis, a serious lung disease. By that time, the family knew that Harold also had the disease. Hannah Nixon took care of Harold at home for a long time. Finally, she took him to live in Arizona, hoping the dry desert

Although he wasn't a natural athlete, Richard (back row, center) worked hard to succeed on the Whittier College football team. This photo was taken in 1933.

The Nixon family went to church three times every Sunday and again on Wednesday evenings.

Richard Nixon began working in his father's gas station and grocery store when he was still a boy. When he was a teenager, he woke up at 4 A.M. each day so he could stock the store's produce counter before he went to school.

air would cure him. While she was away, the other Nixon sons helped their father run the household and the family business. She returned home two years later, in 1933, after Harold died.

By the time his mother returned to California, Richard had graduated from high school. He had done extremely well there, winning prizes in debate and graduating first in his class. After high school, he enrolled in Whittier College. There he continued to earn good grades. He also became a student leader and the president of his class.

After Richard graduated from college, he decided to become a lawyer. His parents did not have enough money to send him to law school, but his good grades earned him a scholarship. This helped him pay his **tuition** to Duke University Law School in North Carolina. He received his law degree in 1937 and returned to California. He went to work in a law office in Whittier.

Richard liked to act, and in his free time, he joined a theater group. There he met a schoolteacher named Thelma Catherine Patricia Ryan. In 1940, Pat Ryan and Richard Nixon married. Two years later, the couple moved to Washington, D.C. One of Nixon's law professors had helped him get a job in the federal government. The United States had just entered World War II, and Richard Nixon's office was in charge of rationing supplies, like food and tires.

Richard Nixon's mother also attended Whittier College.

Richard Nixon and Pat Ryan were married on June 21, 1940.

PAT NIXON

Like her husband, Thelma "Pat" Nixon had a difficult childhood. Her family worked hard but never made much money. "I didn't know what it was not to work hard," she once said. But she remembered good times, too. "It was a good kind of life when you look back on it. I worked right along with my brothers in the fields, which was lots of fun," she recalled.

When Pat was 14, tragedy struck her family. Her mother died, leaving Pat to care for her father and brothers and to tend the house. Two years later, her father became ill. Pat took care of him until his death in 1930. Even with the extra work at home, Pat did very well in school. She dreamed of going to college and of making something of her life. "I wanted to start with an education," she recalled.

Working as a janitor to earn money for school, Pat enrolled at a community college. Then in 1931, an elderly couple asked her to help them move to the East Coast. Pat jumped at the chance to see another part of the country. Once there, she decided to stay in New York. She worked in a hospital until 1934, and then she returned to California and went back to college. After she graduated, Pat became a teacher at Whittier Union High School. Her students admired her friendly personality. She treated her students like adults and enjoyed her work.

In 1937, Pat tried out for a part in a play with the town's theater group. There she met Richard Nixon, who said that for him, "it was love at first sight." Pat wasn't as impressed with Richard at first, but he finally won her heart. They married in 1940.

Over the years, Pat Nixon helped her husband in his political career. When he ran for public office, she helped with the campaign. She always loved to travel, so she went with her husband on trips whenever she could. As first lady, she went with President Nixon to China. She also made trips by herself to Africa and South America. Mrs. Nixon was often praised for her role as a goodwill ambassador, someone who works to improve relations with other countries. Americans also admired her because she volunteered her time to good causes. She encouraged others to volunteer. "You volunteer because you love your country, your people, and because it makes you feel good."

When Richard Nixon resigned from the presidency, Mrs. Nixon publicly supported him. "I have great faith in my husband," she said. "I happen to love him." After the resignation, she became a very private person, preferring a quiet life spent with her family.

"I don't know what history will say about me," Richard Nixon once said, "but I know it will say that Pat Nixon was truly a wonderful woman." Mrs. Nixon died of cancer on June 22, 1993.

EARLY POLITICAL CAREER

In June of 1942, Richard Nixon left the Office of Emergency Management to join the United States Naval Reserve. At first, he was stationed in the United States, but in 1943 he was granted his request to serve in the Pacific. There he worked with the South Pacific Combat Air Transport Command and was in charge of preparing flight plans and loading and unloading cargo planes. Nixon's leadership abilities helped him earn praise and achieve success. By December of 1945, he was back in the United States. He worked as a lawyer in navy offices in several different places.

Nixon's active duty ended in 1946. By that time, he was an active member of the **Republican Party.** Republicans from California had asked Nixon to come back and run for Congress. Nixon thought this sounded like an exciting new

Nixon's leadership skills helped him succeed in the U.S. Navy.

The Nixons had two children: Julie (left) and Tricia (right).

challenge. He and Mrs. Nixon returned to California. As the campaign for Congress began, the Nixons' first child, Patricia (nicknamed Tricia), was born in February of 1946. Their second child, Julie, was born a few years later, in 1948.

Richard Nixon's first campaign has been described as very negative. At that time, many Americans were afraid of **communism.** They believed that the Communist Party in the Soviet Union had plans to take over the world. Some people believed that Americans who had joined the Communist Party were spies and were helping the Soviet Union by revealing American secrets. Nixon claimed that his opponent, Jerry Voorhis, was a communist. It wasn't true. But

Richard Nixon was first nicknamed Tricky Dick during the elections of 1946.

When Nixon was investigating whether Alger Hiss had passed state secrets to a communist, he found evidence that had been hidden in a pumpkin!

Nixon made many people believe it, and this helped him win the election.

After winning the election, the Nixons moved back to Washington, D.C. Communism was a very important topic in the capital city, too. Some members of Congress wanted to investigate those thought to be involved in communist, or "un-American," activities. To investigate people, Congress created the House Un-American Activities Committee. Nixon was **appointed** to this committee during the first year of his **term** in Congress. He led a special investigation on a government worker named Alger Hiss. Mr. Hiss had been accused of passing secret information to a communist spy named Whittaker Chambers. Because

Nixon gained national attention when he investigated a government worker named Alger Hiss for spying. Here Nixon (at right) is shown looking at evidence in the case.

of Nixon's efforts, Hiss was found guilty and was sent to prison for five years. Today historians still argue about whether Hiss was innocent or guilty.

The Hiss investigation made Nixon famous all over the country. He became known as a tough fighter who would do anything to win. In 1950, the Republican Party asked Nixon to run for election to the U.S. Senate. Republican leaders thought he was ready for more responsibility, even though he did not have as much political experience as most senators.

During his campaign for the Senate, Nixon accused his opponent, Helen Gahagan Douglas, of not being tough enough on communists. He said she did not support the House Un-American Activities Committee. Nixon won the election. At age 38, he was the youngest senator at the time.

More success was on the way. Nixon had been a senator for only a year and a half when the Republican Party **nominated** General Dwight D. Eisenhower to run for president in the election of 1952. The Republicans chose Nixon to run for the office of vice president. They hoped he would bring in votes from Westerners and **conservatives.**

By nature, Eisenhower was a quiet, gentle man. He had earned a reputation as a smart and courageous general during World War II. In the election, he said few bad things about the current president, Harry S. Truman. He also refused to say negative things about his opponent from the Democratic Party, Adlai Stevenson.

*In 1952, the Republican Party chose Nixon (at left) as its vice-presidential **candidate** and Dwight D. Eisenhower as its presidential candidate.*

In 1952, Nixon gave what became known as the "Checkers Speech." Nixon talked about his family's dog, Checkers. He said that Checkers was the only gift he had received from Republican Party members while he was a senator. He gained sympathy from Americans when he said, "The kids love that dog, and I want to say right now that regardless of what they say, we're going to keep it."

To win the election, Eisenhower relied on his good reputation and on his promise to end the Korean War. Two years earlier, President Truman had sent U.S. soldiers to fight in South Korea after it was invaded by North Korea. Most Americans wanted the soldiers to come home.

If Eisenhower refused to insult his opponents, Nixon was more than willing to do so. Again, he accused Democratic opponents of not being tough enough on communists. He called Adlai Stevenson "cowardly."

But then, in the middle of the campaign, Nixon was accused of dishonesty. Reporters discovered that while Nixon was a senator, Republicans in California gave him money. A newspaper headline declared, "Secret Rich Men's Trust Fund Keeps Nixon in Style Far Beyond His Salary." The suspicion was that these wealthy Republicans had given Nixon money to influence his votes in Congress. Nixon went on television and admitted he had taken the money. But he explained why: His family could not afford to pay all the expenses he had as a senator. He had used the money to stay in touch with voters back in California. He also pointed out that as senator, he had not done any special favors for the donors. After the speech, many Americans felt Nixon had done nothing wrong. Other people advised Eisenhower to choose someone else to run as the vice-presidential candidate. Instead, when Nixon went to see him, Eisenhower said, "Dick, you're my boy."

Dwight Eisenhower and Richard Nixon easily won the election of 1952. When Eisenhower ran for reelection in 1956, he again chose Nixon as the vice-presidential candidate. Nixon served as vice president for a total of eight years.

Here Nixon is shown with Checkers, the family dog he mentioned in his famous 1952 speech.

While he was vice president, Richard Nixon visited every continent except Antarctica.

Three times during Eisenhower's presidency, Nixon assumed the president's duties when Eisenhower had health problems.

American presidents often give vice presidents little to do, but Eisenhower was different. He asked Nixon to attend **cabinet** meetings. Nixon also sat in on meetings with military advisors. President Eisenhower kept Nixon up-to-date on what was happening in the nation. Nixon often helped Eisenhower make important decisions.

During Eisenhower's presidency, the United States became more and more involved in the Cold War, the growing feelings of distrust between the United States and the Soviet Union. It seemed that a war could erupt at any time between the two nations. Nixon supported Eisenhower's decision to stockpile nuclear arms in case the Soviet Union ever attacked. These dangerous weapons were capable of terrible destruction.

In September of 1955, President Eisenhower had a heart attack while he was on vacation in Colorado. Richard Nixon took on the president's duties while Eisenhower recovered.

THE OFFICE OF VICE PRESIDENT

The U.S. **Constitution** gives the vice president just two responsibilities: to **preside** over the Senate and to cast a ballot in a Senate vote in case of a tie. All vice presidents have fulfilled these duties. Some presidents have also given their vice presidents more to do. Richard Nixon would be one of the most active vice presidents up to that time.

In early American history, the Constitution said the vice president would be the person who came in second in a presidential election. But the 12th Amendment, passed in 1804, said that a **political party** should include on its ticket one candidate for president and another for vice president. For a long time, many vice presidents devoted little time to the job. But when President William Henry Harrison died suddenly in office, his vice president, John Tyler, took over. Americans realized how important the job of vice president could suddenly become. Today vice presidents often run for the office of president when the president leaves office. In recent years, George Bush, Ronald Reagan's vice president, won election to the nation's highest office. Bill Clinton's vice president, Al Gore, ran in the election of 2000, but lost to George W. Bush, son of the former president.

PRESIDENT NIXON

Dwight D. Eisenhower was president for two terms. The law said he could not run for a third term in 1960. When that presidential campaign began, the Republican Party nominated Richard Nixon as their candidate. The Democratic Party nominated John Fitzgerald Kennedy. In the beginning, Kennedy seemed unlikely to win. Many Americans thought he was too young to be president. But Kennedy gained support during the campaign, especially after he and Nixon appeared in a televised debate. Kennedy won the election by a very small number of votes. Out of more than 68 million votes cast, he received only 118,000 more than Nixon.

After Nixon was defeated, he and his family went back to California. He spent most of the next year working on a book called *Six Crises*. He missed politics, however. In 1962, he once again threw his hat in

Nixon ran for president in 1960.

the political ring, this time running for governor of California. He lost that election, too, this one by a large number of votes. At that time it seemed as if Richard Nixon's career in politics was over.

During this period, the political situation in the United States changed rapidly. When President Kennedy was **assassinated** in 1963, vice president Lyndon Baines Johnson became president. At first, Johnson was a very popular president. But during Johnson's second term, the United States became more involved in the war in Vietnam. North Vietnam wanted South Vietnam to become Communist. The U.S. government wanted to keep this from happening. But

While campaigning for Barry Goldwater (the Republican candidate for president in 1964), Nixon visited 36 states. In 1966, he visited 35 states while campaigning for Republicans running for election to Congress.

President Johnson became increasingly unpopular as the Vietnam War dragged on. By 1968, he was exhausted by the situation. He decided not to run for reelection.

Americans began to doubt whether the country should be sending thousands of soldiers to fight communism in a country so far away.

As Johnson continued to struggle with the Vietnam War, he became unpopular. He decided not to run for reelection in 1968. The Democrats nominated Johnson's vice president, Hubert Humphrey, instead. The Republicans chose Richard Nixon. During the campaign, Nixon appealed to conservatives, whom he called the Silent Majority. He said he believed the government wasted too much money. He promised to fight crime. He also promised to end **inflation.**

This was a very difficult time in the United States. Around the country, young people were waging

protests against the Vietnam War. At marches and demonstrations, they displayed signs, chanted slogans, and gave speeches reflecting their belief that the United States should send no more soldiers to fight in the war. Sometimes protests turned violent when police or troops were called in to break them up.

Another source of turmoil in the United States was the **Civil Rights Movement.** For many years, civil rights leaders had been fighting for equal rights for African Americans. They had won some victories, but it was a difficult battle. On April 4, 1968, the Civil

Nixon was the favorite to win the election of 1968. He told people that by voting for him, they were "voting to restore the respect for America." Here he is shown raising his arms in victory after accepting his party's nomination in 1968.

The war in Vietnam was a major political issue while Nixon was running for president. It had become an unpopular war, and many people protested against it.

Rights Movement suffered a terrible blow when one of its most important leaders, Martin Luther King Jr., was assassinated. King had helped keep the movement peaceful, but violence broke out after his death. African Americans rioted across the United States.

Nixon disliked protesters, regardless of what they were fighting against. He believed these people did not respect their country. During his presidential campaign, he promised to bring "peace and order" back to the United States. He avoided talking about the Vietnam War, however. He said only that he would find an "honorable end" to it.

Richard Nixon won the election of 1968 and became president in January of 1969. From the beginning, he was a strong president. Always a loner by nature, he trusted only a few close advisors. He spent a great deal of time alone, reviewing documents and making plans.

President Nixon faced many problems. First, he worked to get the United States out of the Vietnam War. He asked that the government stop **drafting** young men into the military. He also decreased the number of American soldiers in Vietnam. Finally, he decided to end the war by secretly bombing and invading Cambodia and Laos. The United States was not at war with these countries, but the North Vietnamese army was bringing in supplies from them. By bombing them, Nixon closed the supply routes. But the bombings also hurt many innocent people. When news of the bombings spread, new protests began. Many people believed Nixon was making the war bigger instead of ending it as he had

President Nixon believed that people were out to get him. He asked his staff to keep a list of his "enemies." This list included not only his political opponents, but also newspaper reporters, actors, athletes, and businesspeople.

Singer Elvis Presley was a huge fan of President Nixon.

Secretary of State Henry Kissinger (left) was one of Nixon's closest advisors.

promised. One protest ended in tragedy when National Guardsmen fired guns on protesters at Kent State University in Ohio. Four young students were killed.

Peace talks would eventually succeed, and the last American troops would leave Vietnam in 1973. By this time, Nixon had realized that one way to end the war completely was to work with powerful communist

Nixon hoped to end the Vietnam War more quickly, and he secretly ordered the bombing of Laos and Cambodia. Americans were furious about this, believing too many innocent lives had been lost. In response to **criticism** *of his actions, Nixon said, "Those who have power are seldom popular." This antiwar poster encouraged people to protest against Nixon's Vietnam War policies.*

Would you buy a used WAR from this man?

STRIKE! NOV 14
MARCH ON WASHINGTON
& SAN FRANCISCO NOV 15
BRING ALL THE GIS HOME NOW!

countries, such as China and the Soviet Union. These nations supported North Vietnam, so Nixon made a historic visit to China. This opened relations between that country and the United States. Nixon then became the first U.S. president ever to visit the Soviet Union. It began to seem possible that one day, the two countries might not be enemies.

Foreign affairs had taken up most of Nixon's attention during his first term, but he worked on issues at home in the United States as well. He pushed Congress to pass anti-crime laws. He established a new program

NIXON IN CHINA

In 1972, Richard Nixon made history when he visited the People's Republic of China. In the 1950s, the United States and China had a poor relationship because China was a communist country. The United States had worked to prevent China from joining the United Nations, an international organization that works for world peace. The United States had also refused to trade with China. It did not buy goods made in China and refused to sell American goods there. It asked other **democracies** to do the same.

But in 1969, Richard Nixon wanted to build better relations with China. At the time, Chinese leaders were concerned that the Soviet Union might try to invade Asia. They hoped the United States would help prevent this. In 1970, Nixon expressed interest in visiting China. The next spring, members of an American ping-pong team became the first Americans in many years to go there. In June, Secretary of State Henry Kissinger went to Beijing to meet with Chinese leaders. Together they made plans for Nixon to visit.

Richard and Pat Nixon arrived in China on February 22, 1972. Reporters and television camera crews went with them. President Nixon's walk on the Great Wall and his meetings with Chinese leaders were televised. Americans expressed great interest in the country. They admired its beautiful scenery and exotic animals. They were proud of Nixon and hoped that soon the world might become a more peaceful place. "I'm the president that opened relations with China after 25 years of no communication," Nixon once said. His visit to China was one of his most important achievements.

In 1969, astronauts landed on the moon for the first time. President Nixon made the most famous long-distance telephone call in history when he called the astronauts from the White House on July 20, 1969.

Environmentalists organized the first Earth Day on April 22, 1970, during Nixon's first term. All over the country, people gave speeches about protecting the environment and fighting pollution.

to protect the environment. He also supported NASA's space program. In 1969, Americans rejoiced when the United States sent astronauts to the moon in a rocket. The entire country stopped to watch Neil Armstrong walk on the moon.

In 1972, Nixon ran for reelection. His opponent was Democratic Senator George McGovern. In the campaign, Nixon mostly talked about how proud he was to have brought American soldiers home from Vietnam. He won the election by a landslide.

CHAPTER FOUR

NIXON RESIGNS

On January 20, 1973, Richard Nixon was sworn in as president for the second time. In his **inaugural** address, he expressed pride in what he had already accomplished, expressing his view that the world stood "on the threshold of a new era of peace." He reflected on how important it was to the United States that it had improved its relationships with both the Soviet Union and China. He voiced hope that the Vietnam War would soon come to an end. One week later, a **treaty** called the Paris Peace Accords was signed. Although this treaty did not resolve the conflict, it opened the way for the United States to pull all its troops out of Vietnam.

Nixon had a number of successes while he was in office, but acts of dishonesty would soon overshadow his achievements.

Early in his second term, Nixon worked to cut government spending on **welfare,** education, and law enforcement. Cities and states began to share more of these expenses, rather than depending on the national government. To fight inflation, Nixon ordered a price freeze. Companies could not raise prices on their products for a certain period of time. He also placed a tax on foreign goods to encourage Americans to buy things that were made in the United States.

Soon, though, he had little time to devote to making change. Very serious problems developed for the president—and the nation. First, in August, Vice President Spiro T. Agnew was accused of dishonesty. Agnew resigned in October. Gerald R. Ford replaced Agnew as vice president.

Soon the nation learned that Nixon himself was involved in illegal activities. Congress and the FBI became involved in investigating what historians call the Watergate scandal. In June 1972, newspapers had reported that there had been a break-in at the Watergate Hotel, into the offices of the Democratic National Party headquarters. Over the next year, the public learned this was not just an ordinary burglary.

During the 1972 presidential campaign, a break-in occurred at the Democratic National Headquarters' offices (below). It later was discovered that President Nixon's own advisors had ordered the break-in.

This political cartoon shows President Nixon as Pinocchio, the storybook character whose nose grew whenever he lied. Nixon's nose is very long in the cartoon, indicating he was lying when he said he knew nothing about the Watergate break-in.

During the 1972 presidential campaign, Republicans had played "dirty tricks" on the Democrats to help Nixon win the election. For one thing, the Republican Committee for the Reelection of the President used illegal gifts of money to find out what the Democrats were planning. It was President Nixon's own advisors who had hired five men to break into the Democrats' office. Once inside, they hoped to steal information about their opponents' campaign plans. They also planned to place a device in the office that would allow them to listen to the Democrats' phone calls. Nixon's aides hoped this would help him win reelection.

*James McCord (right) was an electronics expert involved in the Watergate break-in. Here he is shown speaking at the Senate Watergate Hearings about **bugging devices** planted during the break-in.*

The first president to be impeached was Andrew Johnson, who found himself in trouble after he fired a government official. In 1868, Congress began an impeachment trial, arguing that this was not Johnson's right and that he had committed a crime in firing the man. The Senate was one vote short of **convicting** Johnson of the charges, however, and he remained president.

For a time, Americans believed President Nixon when he said that he knew nothing about what happened at the Watergate Hotel. They soon lost trust in him, however. The public learned that even if Nixon did not plan the theft, he had to have known about it. Nixon tried to cover it up, or hide the truth. He did not want Americans to find out about his role in the scandal.

When rumors of the cover-up reached the Senate, its members appointed investigators to look into the matter. The investigators found out that Nixon had used tape recorders in his office. Nixon had recorded all conversations held there. The investigators pressed the president to give them the tapes of his conversations about the Watergate scandal. In April of 1974, Nixon released **transcripts** of the tapes, but some information had been removed. Nixon did not want to release the tapes themselves, but the Supreme Court ordered him to do so a few months later, on July 24.

The tapes proved that President Nixon knew about the Watergate burglary. Even worse, they proved that Nixon had ordered the cover-up. When members of Congress realized Nixon had covered up the crime, he lost all support. Even his oldest political friends refused to help him. Congress wanted to **impeach** the president. This meant he would face a trial in the Senate.

Nixon knew that if he were impeached, he would almost certainly be found guilty and be forced to step down from the presidency. Before impeachment proceedings could begin, President Nixon decided to resign. On August 8, 1974, he went on television and announced his decision. The next day, he wrote a letter to the secretary of state formally stating his resignation. He and his family then boarded a helicopter on the White

The second president to be impeached was Bill Clinton, who faced impeachment hearings in 1998. He was found not guilty of the charges against him.

On August 9, 1974, the day after he resigned, President Nixon left the White House by helicopter.

Richard Nixon was never charged with a crime, but other members of his staff were. Seven people were accused of interfering with the investigation into the Watergate Scandal. Three went to jail.

Many Americans disagreed with President Ford's decision to pardon Richard Nixon. Ford believed that was the right thing to do for the country. Still, many historians believe that one reason Ford was not elected president in 1976 was because he had pardoned Nixon.

House lawn and flew home to California. That same day, Gerald Ford was sworn in as the new president.

On September 8, 1974, President Ford signed a letter granting Richard Nixon a **pardon.** This meant that Richard Nixon could not be tried for any crimes.

Richard Nixon lived for 20 years after he resigned from the presidency. He tried hard to regain the respect of Americans. He went on speaking tours and wrote books about foreign affairs. He offered other presidents advice about U.S. relations with other countries. He also traveled around the world to meet with foreign leaders. In 1990, the Nixon Presidential Library opened. It later became part of the National Archives.

In recent years, books about Richard Nixon have criticized him for Watergate. But they have also praised him for his achievements as a statesman. On April 22, 1994, shortly after a final trip to the Soviet Union and completing his 11th book, Richard Nixon died at the age of 81. Newspapers published obituaries that talked about both his accomplishments and his failings.

Five U.S. presidents attended Richard Nixon's funeral (from left to right): Bill Clinton, George H.W. Bush, Ronald Reagan, Jimmy Carter, and Gerald Ford.

NIXON TAPES

In 1971, Richard Nixon had a secret taping system installed in the White House. Microphones were placed in the Oval Office and other places. His telephone conversations were also recorded. For the most part, the people he talked to did not know he was recording them. Over the years, close to 4,000 hours of his conversations would be recorded.

It was during the Watergate scandal that reporters and government officials found out about these tapes. Transcripts—written records of what had been said—of some of his conversations were introduced as evidence in the Watergate hearings. But they were only a small part of what had been recorded.

After his resignation, Richard Nixon worked hard to keep these tapes private. He did not want anyone to hear what was on them. But after a lawsuit was filed by a historian who argued that the public had the right to know what happened while Nixon was president, the National Archives agreed to start making the tapes public.

TIME LINE

1913
Richard Milhous Nixon is born on January 9 in Yorba Linda, California.

1922
The Nixon family moves from Yorba Linda to the nearby town of Whittier, where Frank Nixon opens a gas station.

1930
Nixon graduates from high school and enrolls at Whittier College.

1937
Nixon graduates from the law school at Duke University and begins his career as an attorney.

1940
Richard Nixon marries Pat Ryan.

1942
Nixon is appointed an attorney for the U.S. Office of Emergency Management. He and Pat move to Washington, D.C. Within a few months, he leaves his job to join the navy.

1946
The Nixons have their first child, a daughter named Patricia. Nixon is elected to the U.S. House of Representatives.

1948
Julie, the Nixons' second daughter, is born.

1950
Nixon runs for election to the Senate and wins.

1952
Dwight Eisenhower runs for president with Nixon as the vice-presidential candidate. Nixon is accused of accepting money and gifts from wealthy Republicans. He appears on national television, saying that he took money only to help pay his campaign expenses. Eisenhower and Nixon win the election.

1955
Richard Nixon assumes the president's responsibilities when Eisenhower becomes sick.

1956
Eisenhower and Nixon are reelected.

1960
Richard Nixon runs for election as president but loses to John F. Kennedy.

1962
Nixon loses the election for governor of California.

1963
President Kennedy is assassinated on November 22. Vice President Lyndon Baines Johnson becomes president.

1968
Civil rights leader Martin Luther King Jr. is assassinated on April 4, leading to violent protests. Nixon is elected president of the United States in November.

1969
On July 20, *Apollo 11* astronaut Neil Armstrong becomes the first person to walk on the moon, winning the "space race" for the United States. Millions of people around the world watch the moon landing on television.

1970
Environmentalists organize the first Earth Day on April 22. Nixon secretly bombs North Vietnam's supply routes in Cambodia and Laos, killing many innocent people. On May 4, four students are killed during an antiwar protest at Kent State University in Ohio.

1971
Nixon announces that he will visit the People's Republic of China, stunning the world because he had long been firmly opposed to communism. The Nixons' daughter Tricia marries Edward Cox at the White House.

1972
Nixon visits China in February, opening relations between the two countries for the first time since China became a communist country in 1949. In May, Nixon becomes the first U.S. president to visit the Soviet Union. In June, burglars break into Democratic Party headquarters to steal information to help Nixon win reelection. When the burglars are caught, Nixon and other officials try to cover up their involvement in the scandal. Nixon wins the election in November, defeating Democrat George McGovern.

1973
The last American troops leave Vietnam. Americans learn about the Watergate scandal.

1974
Throughout the winter and spring, Congress investigates Nixon's involvement in the Watergate burglary. Nixon avoids giving information to investigators. In April, he releases edited transcripts of his conversations in the Oval Office, but much of the information has been removed. On July 24, the Supreme Court rules that Nixon must turn over all the tapes. On August 5, he releases tapes that prove he knew about the burglary and that he tried to cover it up. On August 8, Richard Nixon announces to the American people that he will resign. Gerald Ford is sworn in as the new president on August 9. Ford pardons Nixon in September.

1990
The Nixon presidential library opens. Richard Nixon is honored when four other presidents attend the ceremony.

1993
Pat Nixon dies on June 22.

1994
Richard Nixon dies on April 22.

GLOSSARY

appointed (uh-POYN-ted) When someone is appointed, he or she is asked by an important official to accept a position. Nixon was appointed to the House Un-American Activities Committee.

assassinated (uh-SASS-ih-nay-tid) Assassinated means murdered. President Kennedy was assassinated in 1963.

bugging devices (BUG-ing di-VY-sez) Bugging devices are microphones that are hidden in a room so that people in another place can hear what people are saying in that room. Burglars planted bugging devices at the Democratic National Headquarters in 1972.

cabinet (KAB-ih-net) A cabinet is the group of people who advise a president. President Eisenhower invited Nixon to attend cabinet meetings.

campaign (kam-PAYN) A campaign is the process of running for an election, including activities such as giving speeches or attending rallies. Pat Nixon helped with her husband's campaigns.

candidate (KAN-dih-det) A candidate is a person running in an election. The Republican Party asked Nixon to become a candidate in the 1946 election for Congress.

Civil Rights Movement (SIV-el RYTZ MOOV-ment) The Civil Rights Movement was the struggle for equal rights for African Americans in the United States during the 1950s and 1960s. Martin Luther King Jr. was an important leader of the Civil Rights Movement.

communism (KOM-yoo-niz-em) Communism is a system of government in which the central government, not the people, holds all the power. Many Americans were afraid of communism after World War II.

conservatives (kuhn-SUR-vuh-tivs) In politics, conservatives are people who oppose radical change and like things to stay as they are or used to be. Nixon appealed to conservatives during the 1968 election.

constitution (kon-stih-TOO-shun) A constitution is the set of basic principles that govern a country. The U.S. Constitution describes the duties of the nation's leaders.

convicting (kuhn-VIK-ting) Convicting means finding or proving that someone is guilty of a crime. When President Andrew Johnson was impeached, the Senate was one vote short of convicting him.

criticism (KRIT-uh-siz-im) Criticism is the act of telling someone what he or she has done wrong. Nixon tried to ignore criticism of his actions.

democracies (deh-MOK-ruh-seez) Democracies are nations in which the people control the government by electing their own leaders. The United States is a democracy.

Democratic Party (dem-uh-KRAT-ik PAR-tee) The Democratic Party is one of the two major political parties in the United States. The Democratic Party opposed Nixon's party, the Republican Party.

drafting (DRAFT-ing) When a nation is drafting people, it is requiring them to serve in the armed forces. President Nixon asked the government to stop drafting men into the military in an attempt to stop the Vietnam War.

environmentalists (en-vye-ruhn-MEN-tuhl-ists) Environmentalists are people interested in protecting the environment. Environmentalists established Earth Day during Nixon's presidency.

impeach (im-PEECH) When Congress impeaches a president or vice president, it is voting to charge him or her with a crime or serious misdeed. Nixon avoided impeachment by resigning from office.

inaugural (ih-NAWG-yuh-ruhl) Inaugural refers to the ceremony that takes place when a new president begins a term. In his second inaugural address, Nixon referred to the accomplishments of his first term.

inflation (in-FLAY-shun) Inflation is a sharp and sudden rise in the price of goods. During his 1968 campaign, Nixon promised to end inflation in the United States.

nominated (NOM-ih-nay-tid) If a political party nominated someone, it chose that person to run for a political office. The Republican Party nominated Nixon to run for president in the 1968 election.

pardon (PAR-don) If a leader pardons someone, he or she excuses that person for crimes or misdeeds. President Gerald Ford pardoned Richard Nixon.

political party (puh-LIT-ih-kul PAR-tee) A political party is a group of people who share similar ideas about how to run a government. Nixon was a member of the Republican political party.

politics (PAWL-ih-tiks) Politics refers to the actions and practices of the government. As a young man, Nixon became interested in politics.

preside (pre-ZYD) If someone presides over a meeting, he or she is in charge of it. The vice president presides over sessions in the Senate.

protests (PROH-tests) Protests are gatherings at which people speak out against something they believe is wrong. In the 1960s, many young people took part in protests against the Vietnam War.

Republican Party (re-PUB-lih-kin PAR-tee) The Republican Party is one of two major political parties in the United States. Richard Nixon was a member of the Republican Party.

resign (ree-ZINE) When a person resigns from a job, he or she gives it up. Nixon was the first president of the United States to resign from office.

scandal (SKAN-dul) A scandal is a shameful action that shocks the public. The Watergate scandal involved President Nixon.

Soviet Union (SOH-vee-et YOON-yen) The Soviet Union was a communist country that stretched from eastern Europe across Asia to the Pacific Ocean. It separated into several smaller countries in 1991.

term (TERM) A term is the length of time a politician can keep his or her position by law. Nixon served on the House Un-American Committee during his term in Congress.

transcripts (TRAN-skriptz) Transcripts are written records of what was said in a conversation or interview. Nixon released transcripts of the taped Watergate scandal conversations in 1974.

treaty (TREE-tee) A treaty is a formal agreement between nations. Nixon helped negotiate a treaty that paved the way for the withdrawal of U.S. troops from Vietnam.

tuition (too-ISH-un) Tuition is the fee for going to a school. Nixon's good grades earned him a scholarship, which helped pay his tuition to law school.

welfare (WELL-fayr) Welfare is aid provided by the government to people in need. Nixon reduced government spending on welfare programs.

THE UNITED STATES GOVERNMENT

The United States government is divided into three equal branches: the executive, the legislative, and the judicial. This division helps prevent abuses of power because each branch has to answer to the other two. No one branch can become too powerful.

EXECUTIVE BRANCH

PRESIDENT
VICE PRESIDENT
DEPARTMENTS

The job of the executive branch is to enforce the laws. It is headed by the president, who serves as the spokesperson for the United States around the world. The president signs bills into law and appoints important officials such as federal judges. He or she is also the commander in chief of the U.S. military. The president is assisted by the vice president, who takes over if the president dies or cannot carry out the duties of the office.

The executive branch also includes various departments, each focused on a specific topic. They include the Defense Department, the Justice Department, and the Agriculture Department. The department heads, along with other officials such as the vice president, serve as the president's closest advisers, called the cabinet.

LEGISLATIVE BRANCH

CONGRESS
*Senate and
House of Representatives*

The job of the legislative branch is to make the laws. It consists of Congress, which is divided into two parts: the Senate and the House of Representatives. The Senate has 100 members, and the House of Representatives has 435 members. Each state has two senators. The number of representatives a state has varies depending on the state's population.

Besides making laws, Congress also passes budgets and enacts taxes. In addition, it is responsible for declaring war, maintaining the military, and regulating trade with other countries.

JUDICIAL BRANCH

SUPREME COURT
COURTS OF APPEALS
DISTRICT COURTS

The job of the judicial branch is to interpret the laws. It consists of the nation's federal courts. Trials are held in district courts. During trials, judges must decide what laws mean and how they apply. Courts of appeals review the decisions made in district courts.

The nation's highest court is the Supreme Court. If someone disagrees with a court of appeals ruling, he or she can ask the Supreme Court to review it. The Supreme Court may refuse. The Supreme Court makes sure that decisions and laws do not violate the Constitution.

CHOOSING
THE PRESIDENT

It may seem odd, but American voters don't elect the president directly. Instead, the president is chosen using what is called the Electoral College.

Each state gets as many votes in the Electoral College as its combined total of senators and representatives in Congress. For example, Iowa has two senators and five representatives, so it gets seven electoral votes. Although the District of Columbia does not have any voting members in Congress, it gets three electoral votes. Usually, the candidate who wins the most votes in any given state receives all of that state's electoral votes.

To become president, a candidate must get more than half of the Electoral College votes. There are a total of 538 votes in the Electoral College, so a candidate needs 270 votes to win. If nobody receives 270 Electoral College votes, the House of Representatives chooses the president.

With the Electoral College system, the person who receives the most votes nationwide does not always receive the most electoral votes. This happened most recently in 2000, when Al Gore received half a million more national votes than George W. Bush. Bush became president because he had more Electoral College votes.

THE WHITE HOUSE

The White House is the official home of the president of the United States. It is located at 1600 Pennsylvania Avenue NW in Washington, D.C. In 1792, a contest was held to select the architect who would design the president's home. James Hoban won. Construction took eight years.

The first president, George Washington, never lived in the White House. The second president, John Adams, moved into the house in 1800, though the inside was not yet complete. During the War of 1812, British soldiers burned down much of the White House. It was rebuilt several years later.

The White House was changed through the years. Porches were added, and President Theodore Roosevelt added the West Wing. President William Taft changed the shape of the presidential office, making it into the famous Oval Office. While Harry Truman was president, the old house was discovered to be structurally weak. All the walls were reinforced with steel, and the rooms were rebuilt.

Today, the White House has 132 rooms (including 35 bathrooms), 28 fireplaces, and 3 elevators. It takes 570 gallons of paint to cover the outside of the six-story building. The White House provides the president with many ways to relax. It includes a putting green, a jogging track, a swimming pool, a tennis court, and beautifully landscaped gardens. The White House also has a movie theater, a billiard room, and a one-lane bowling alley.

PRESIDENTIAL PERKS

The job of president of the United States is challenging. It is probably one of the most stressful jobs in the world. Because of this, presidents are paid well, though not nearly as well as the leaders of large corporations. In 2007, the president earned $400,000 a year. Presidents also receive extra benefits that make the demanding job a little more appealing.

★ **Camp David:** In the 1940s, President Franklin D. Roosevelt chose this heavily wooded spot in the mountains of Maryland to be the presidential retreat, where presidents can relax. Even though it is a retreat, world business is conducted there. Most famously, President Jimmy Carter met with Middle Eastern leaders at Camp David in 1978. The result was a peace agreement between Israel and Egypt.

★ *Air Force One:* The president flies on a jet called *Air Force One.* It is a Boeing 747-200B that has been modified to meet the president's needs.

Air Force One is the size of a large home. It is equipped with a dining room, sleeping quarters, a conference room, and office space. It also has two kitchens that can provide food for up to 50 people.

★ **The Secret Service:** While not the most glamorous of the president's perks, the Secret Service is one of the most important. The Secret Service is a group of highly trained agents who protect the president and the president's family.

★ **The Presidential State Car:** The presidential limousine is a stretch Cadillac DTS.

It has been armored to protect the president in case of attack. Inside the plush car are a foldaway desk, an entertainment center, and a communications console.

★ **The Food:** The White House has five chefs who will make any food the president wants. The White House also has an extensive wine collection.

★ **Retirement:** A former president receives a pension, or retirement pay, of just under $180,000 a year. Former presidents also receive Secret Service protection for the rest of their lives.

FACTS

QUALIFICATIONS

To run for president, a candidate must

- ★ be at least 35 years old
- ★ be a citizen who was born in the United States
- ★ have lived in the United States for 14 years

TERM OF OFFICE

A president's term of office is four years.
No president can stay in office for more than two terms.

ELECTION DATE

The presidential election takes place every four years on the first Tuesday of November.

INAUGURATION DATE

Presidents are inaugurated on January 20.

OATH OF OFFICE

I do solemnly swear I will faithfully execute the office of the President of the United States and will to the best of my ability preserve, protect, and defend the Constitution of the United States.

WRITE A LETTER TO THE PRESIDENT

One of the best things about being a U.S. citizen is that Americans get to participate in their government. They can speak out if they feel government leaders aren't doing their jobs. They can also praise leaders who are going the extra mile. Do you have something you'd like the president to do? Should the president worry more about the environment and encourage people to recycle? Should the government spend more money on our schools? You can write a letter to the president to say how you feel!

1600 Pennsylvania Avenue
Washington, D.C. 20500
You can even send an e-mail to: president@whitehouse.gov

BOOKS

Anderson, Dale. *Watergate: Scandal in the White House.* Minneapolis: Compass Point Books, 2007.

Aronson, Billy. *Richard M. Nixon.* New York: Marshall Cavendish Children's Books, 2008.

Harris, Bill. *The First Ladies Fact Book.* New York: Black Dog & Leventhal Publishers, 2005.

Levy, Debbie. *The Vietnam War.* Minneapolis: Lerner Publications, 2004.

Ochester, Betsy. *Richard M. Nixon: America's 37th President.* New York: Children's Press, 2005.

Santella, Andrew. *Impeachment.* New York: Children's Press, 2000.

VIDEOS

The American President. DVD, VHS (Alexandria, VA: PBS Home Video, 2000).

Biography: Richard Nixon. DVD (New York: A & E Home Video, 2005).

The History Channel Presents The Presidents. DVD (New York: A & E Home Video, 2005).

National Geographic's Inside the White House. DVD (Washington, D.C.: National Geographic Video, 2003).

Nixon. VHS (Alexandria, VA: PBS Home Video, 1990).

INTERNET SITES

Visit our Web page for lots of links about Richard M. Nixon and other U.S. presidents:

http://www.childsworld.com/links

Note to Parents, Teachers, and Librarians: We routinely verify our Web links to make sure they are safe, active sites—so encourage your readers to check them out!

INDEX